VIRGINIA

A play by

Edna O'Brien

1981

THE HOGARTH PRESS

LONDON

Published by
The Hogarth Press
40 William IV Street
London WC2N 4DF

*

Clark, Irwin & Co Ltd
Toronto

British Library Cataloguing
in Publication Data

O'Brien, Edna
  Virginia.
  1. English drama—Irish authors
  1. Title
  822.9'14   PR6029.B/

ISBN 0 7012 0539 3

Printed in Great Britain by
T. H. Brickell & Son Ltd., The Blackmore Press,
Shaftesbury, Dorset.

To
NIGEL NICOLSON

The Characters

VIRGINIA appears as a grown woman and also as her youthful self. Her mode of talking varies drastically. She is at times quick, high-spirited; other times ruminative and once like a somnambulist. She talks to THE MAN, to herself, and to the audience and when she is talking her 'writing' it is in another vein altogether—reflective, rapturous, dreamlike.

THE MAN appears first as an old man—her father. He wears a greatcoat and in his several pockets there is a book. He always has a book to hand and is often seen to be muttering under his breath. The mutter is inaudible, it is this:
"But I beneath a rougher sea
Was whelmed in deeper gulf."
Next he is LEONARD WOOLF. There is a notable contrast in his first appearance as LEONARD, when he strides in, full of vigour, like any young man about to propose to any young woman. In later scenes he has a pronounced tremor.

VITA appears as a dashing woman of 37, regal bearing, with bohemian manners. She is sensuality as opposed to VIRGINIA's etherealness.

It is an abstract set. Projected on screens throughout the play are various shots of Bloomsbury, London streets, the country etc.

ACT ONE

Scene One

MAN: I ask myself why this ecstasy, why this terror—what is it that fills me with extraordinary excitement.

VIRGINIA: I dreamt that I leant over the edge of the boat and fell down. I went under the sea, I have been dead and yet am now alive again—it was awful, awful, and as before waking, the voices of the birds and the sound of wheels chime and chatter in a queer harmony, grow louder and louder and the sleeper feels himself drawing towards the shores of life, the sun growing hotter, cries sounding louder, something tremendous about to happen.

MAN: Ginny—Virginia!

[VIRGINIA *looks at him with withheld rage.*]

VIRGINIA: Moments, moments of my being . . . in here, captive. I shall scrape the sea-bed clean. My father bent over his tomes . . . no light lover he, no superficial optimist, one of the giant breed, alone in the ice-bound seas.

My two bloods dashing together My father's scrutinous, bold, brutal, an oarsman, coach of oarsmen. And my mother's decorous, beautiful and afraid.

His wife my mother. When she was presiding it was all very moving and very stirring, the room full of people, her several children, the nursery ceiling very high and plates and plates of innocent bread and butter.

Life and a little strip of time presented itself to her eyes to her fifty years. She took a look at life, and she had a clear sense of it, something real, something private which she shared neither with her children

9

nor her husband. She was always trying to get the better of it as it was of her and sometimes they parleyed, she felt this thing called Life terrible, hostile and quick to pounce on you. And then she said brandishing her sword "Nonsense."

Yes I wanted her to myself, one does. I wanted to be singled out. I would show her my little stories about souls flying about looking for bodies. She liked that. My mother, his wife, not at all the same thing. It must be a strange thing to be man and wife, all that copulation. Marriage and motherhood without awakenment. It is not enough. Rather crowded and rather anxious and very valiant but it is not enough. Her pride in him was like the pride of one in some lofty mountain peak visited only by the light of the stars, noble, yes, enthusiastic, yes, but humble, too humble. My mother. One says it. One cannot not say it. A single phrase, or her voice, or that beautiful figure so upright in the ground, in her long shabby cloak, the head held high, so upright and so distinct and the eyes that looked straight ahead, hurrying saying,

"Come along, quick, quick, don't keep Father waiting."

Or sitting there writing a letter at the table, and the silver candlesticks and the high carved chair and the three cornered brass inkpot and then not there.

She was upstairs and my half-brother, George Duckworth took me into her bedroom to kiss her goodbye and she said, "Hold yourself straight my little goat."

It was May the fifth, eighteen ninety five.

It was about six in the morning. I saw the doctor walk away, I saw the pigeons floating, settling.

They wrapped towels around me and gave me brandy, I think the sun was coming up. She had just died.

ACT ONE

Death plays havoc.

MAN: No, no, no.

VIRGINIA: [*resistant*] No, no.

END OF SCENE ONE

ACT ONE

Scene Two

VIRGINIA: We rallied, my sister and I, we rallied. That was the thing. That was the supreme test. My father, bent, unstrung, saying the same thing over and over again.

MAN: I never told her I never told her how much I loved her. REPEATED SEVERAL TIMES

VIRGINIA: The house was full of mourners, women, pathos, bathos.
The black-edged letter paper so thick that there was no room for the message. He had not told her that he loved her. The old story. Too late.

MAN: I was not as bad as Carlyle, was I.

VIRGINIA: He wants comfort but what comfort can we give.

MAN: Everyone has forgotten me.

VIRGINIA: A skinless man and skinless children.
Let him be fifty feet away, let him not even speak, not even see you, he permeated, he prevailed, he demanded, one pretended to drink from a cup to escape his demands, to put aside a moment longer that imperious need . . . Do this, do that . . . his dominance, his "Submit to me."
The words wrote themselves, leaf upon leaf, fold upon fold, incessant, upon the brain.
For no one attracted me more, his hands were beautiful to me and his feet, and his voice and his words, and his haste and his temper and his oddity and his passion, and his saying straight out before everyone

MAN: "We perish each alone,"

VIRGINIA: And his remoteness.

13

VIRGINIA

A discredit to stand there and be sexually dumb. One said.

MAN: What did one say?

VIRGINIA: Crushed and cranked in the womb by your important works and now having to be grown up and tell you that you are not as bad as Mr. Carlyle. So selfish, such inconceivable selfishness.

Hate rising up in me against him, sharpening, sharpening.

Does it spread to all other men. Men in conflict for the different parts of my body. So selfish and so stingy. When my sister Nessa asked for the housekeeping money he said she should be ashamed of herself and that she would make us bankrupt. No wonder I had tantrums *and* fidgets.

"Nor will in fading silks compose faintly the inimitable rose . . . "

Along with that, my sister and I had to come out. To Come Out on nothing. That silly world of white satin and kid gloves and visiting cards and young men from the Foreign Office who never heard of Plato but who could dance. The man or the woman who shines at a dance is at the centre of things. Lord Gayton and Nancy Blowe—they met, they danced and that was it. So clear, so clever, such enormous resources.

MAN: To be them would be marvellous but she is condemned to be herself. By some malice of fate she is unable to join in.

VIRGINIA: Eros came on dirty wings. My half brother George was taking me to Lady Sligo's Ball.

My dress was made of green stuff bought at a furniture shop because it was cheaper and also more adventurous. The brougham waiting, the pavement silver in the new moon, half insane with shyness and with nervousness, I entered the Ball . . . And gallopaded around the room discussing oratory and

14

the Garter with young men from the Foreign Office. Dancing, feeling the queerness and the strangeness of being alone with a complete stranger, striking out this way and that like a beginner on ice. My half brother danced with all the ladies and then bowed to them then brought me home.

I went up to my bedroom, unfastened the brooch that he gave me and then; the door opened and in the dark someone entered—"Who", I cried. "Don't be frightened," George replied, "and don't turn on the light, oh beloved."

He flung himself on my bed and took me in his arms. Something in him burst, reticence you could say or decency or etiquette, the things that middle class men are supposed to possess. "Besides I love you, I must have you," he said.

The division in our lives was most curious. There was my father in the next room teaching me the humanities and the sciences the rules against error. All theory, Vapid, Theory.

I am unlearned. Make no mistake the Greeks are for men, the Treasury is for men, Whitehall is for men, the world belongs to men.

[*She looks at the* MAN]

I wanted a mind, a man, a sparring partner, but they were all in Cambridge. My brother Toby was in Cambridge.

If the spirit of peace dwelt anywhere it was in those rooms in Cambridge those courts, those quadrangles, colours burning in the windowpane like the beat of an excitable heart . . . all the books and smoke and drink and deep armchairs . . . the urbanity.

MAN: The geniality.

VIRGINIA: The dignity.

MAN: The privacy.

VIRGINIA: [*Ignoring him*] My brother Toby knew the

15

most interesting fellows apostles and geniuses. [*very excited*] Lytton Strachey a wit, Sydney Turner another, slept all day and read all night, Woolf a strange wild man, a Jew, Clive Bell an atheist and what is more a muscular atheist, who not only wrote peoms but had Edna May to lunch in his rooms, dammit, while we famished at home and tackled Greek and did bookbinding and laid the table and were polite to women, to Aunts, women in constant lacrimous attendance for every death and every deathknock.

MAN: Ginia you are such a comfort to me, so good to me.

VIRGINIA: If you must die, why don't you.

[VIRGINIA *turns as if she is about to recall him but doesn't. She crosses and snaps closed the book that he was reading.*]

VIRGINIA: His life would have entirely ended mine—no writing, no rooks slicing the air, no stories, inconceivable.

It was a question of throwing out all the old things, the stacks of letters, the pictures, the Past and moving to Gordon Square. It was a most beautiful thing to have distempered walls and bright chintzes, to have coffee instead of tea.

And Nessa and I no longer in white satin but in coloured dresses like Gaugin painted.

And so began our Thursdays. The bell would ring after dinner and in they glided, Strachey, and Sydney Turner and Leonard Woolf and Clive Bell. Clive Bell, a mixture between Shelley and a country squire, Lytton Strachey. [*adoringly*]

The Strache, with a passion for Pope. So thin, his thigh no thicker than my arm, saying [*ponderous voice*]

"Do you hear the music of the spheres," and then

16

fainting; and Sydney Turner who only spoke the truth, the absolute truth.

And I had to hide the matchboxes because they clashed with the colours.

They would settle themselves in corners and gaze into the distance and for a long time say nothing.

"No,"

"No, I have not seen it,"

"No, I have not been there,"

"No I do not agree."

Until they got on to something really interesting such as beauty or whether intimacy led to a dust of the soul.

Every word had an aura. Poetry combined the different auras in a sequence.

But is it founded upon texture or upon structure.

I would think I am a story, he is a story, she is a story, but how to get it. Not just the theory and the argument, holding the thing—all the things—the innumerable things together. Phrases for the moon, how people looked, turned, dropped their cigarette ends. And then Strachey who hadn't spoken for ages suddenly said, "Semen," looking at a stain on Nessa's skirt. "Semen. Deplorable, deplorable, as Henry James would say." "Semen—Can one say it," and then suddenly we were all laughing. Nessa laughed the most. How beautiful she was and how ready. Astride her Arab mare—I mean life. She was the sunlight and I was the twilight. Love was not mentioned. Anyhow the great artist was Androgenous. I had known that there were buggers in Plato's Greece but it never occured to me that there could be buggers in our drawing room in forty six Gordon Square.

James is in despair, Rupert has been twice jilted, Morgan isn't coping.

17

VIRGINIA

Love and marriage was a lowdown affair and yet

> [*reciting*]
> "Miss Buss and Mr. Beale
> Cupid's darts do feel."

I never dreamed it would happen.
Nessa put her arms above her head and said "I can see that we shall marry." I could feel the fate that would descend and snatch us apart, we who had been drawn together as though by some capilliary attraction, we who had ruled the world between us.
> [*crisply*]
> "Marry? Who?"

VIRGINIA: [*as* NESSA] "Who ever."

VIRGINIA: "Marry? Our father not long dead and you talk of marry."
Women are hard to women. Women dislike women.
[*to* NESSA] "It's indecent . . . Marry . . . ? Who?"

VIRGINIA: [*as* NESSA] "Clive, for instance."

VIRGINIA: [*as herself*] "He is not good enough. A jerky little man who chases girls. He even discusses modern verse with a jerk." [*addressing him*] "You are all sensitive appreciations Mr. Bell, but you have no character, you lack bottom." [*To* NESSA] "He blushes like a sunset and blinks like a windmill." [*To the Audience*] I couldn't stop her, she began to put roses behind her ear and wear the pink cloak that we bought on our travels in Constantinople. She began seeing him every day. I would have to come between them because she was everything to me . . . she was mother, father, brother, sister, lover.

VIRGINIA: So it was another move for my brother Adrian and me, if I were to get any good from her marriage and believe me I meant to. It was then I hatched my little plan.
To come between them. Jealousy at the bottom of it.

18

ACT ONE

Jealousy which survives every other passion of mankind.

Oh Clive, I am so palpitating, I am so affectionate, I cannot write a novel, because I cannot find the right pen, and Clive, if we go for another walk shall I come in woollies?

He was someone to make the afternoons hum. I would rub up his wits and in return get my manners polished. How we talked, a plethora of talk, about the elephants in Kent or potted tongue or Rousseau or Madame de Stael or whether it was colder in the eighteenth century or why the Russians had no sense of humour. And she would be left at home to mind their baby. I believe he hated that baby . . . as I believe I did . . . he and I had that in common, we hated babies and Nessa loved them. She clapped when it burped. [sarcastically]

And as for babies wonderful plops and no sign of measles touch wood. "Clive, what is the origin of touch wood?" And he would take down the encyclopaedia and one day he said to me, he said "Virginia what is the brightest thing you can think of?" And I said, "A leaf with a light on it." and I meant it. She saw us go arm in arm across the downs. Then one day she called me aside—it was after the three of us had been to Florence—and she was so kind about it, but that was because she was hurt. She said "Now Virginia, we know it's not true, we all know that it's not true but your Aunts would say that you are flirting with my husband." And then she said "If you had loved him, I would not mind so much, but you do not love him."

[VIRGINIA *flounces away as if from her sister and is haughty.*]

VIRGINIA: Love, there is something faintly ridiculous about it. [*reciting*]

19

VIRGINIA

How different from us, Mr. Beale
And Miss Buss.
[*Barrel Organ*]
Far preferable to go out into the London street and
toss my brain in the air. What a lark, what a plunge,
how fresh, how calm the air, June, June that draws
out every leaf on every tree. Mothers of Pimlico
giving suck to their young.
Messages passing from the Fleet to the Admiralty.
Arlington Street and Piccadilly seemed to chaff the
very air . . . London gay and defiant.
Ah Mr. Woolf. I hear you have done wonders in
Ceylon, governing natives, shooting tigers, hanging
blacks.

LEONARD: I'm glad to be home.

VIRGINIA: Tell me something about Ceylon, something
I don't know.

LEONARD: One day I was travelling by train and there
were all those dead sharks on the seashore and they
all had this strange smile, this strange smirk.

VIRGINIA: [*disbelieving*] Really. And what do you do
since you came home?

LEONARD: I cycle about, I see my old friends from Cambridge . . . I go for walks, I discuss G. E. Moore.

VIRGINIA: Still?

LEONARD: I've been to the Zoo. The lions behave as if
they had been born in South Kensington.

VIRGINIA: How, how?

LEONARD: I saw a curious incident. The lions were in
their indoor cages. A stout, middle-aged, middle-
class lady was standing near the bars looking at a
magnificent lion who was standing on the other side
of the bars gazing over her head, as lions seem to do,
into eternity. Suddenly he turned round, presented
his backside to her and pissed on her through the

20

bars. "Oh the dirty beast," she said. "Oh the dirty beast."

VIRGINIA: [*laughing*] Oh the dirty beast.
[*she laughs and then suddenly stops*]
That's a stupid thing, haven't you anything better to say.

LEONARD: Yes. [*Pause*] Marry me.

VIRGINIA: [*aside*] Why does everyone talk of marriage—is it crude human nature breaking out?

LEONARD: It is true that I am cold and reserved to other people.

VIRGINIA: According to yourself.

LEONARD: I am selfish, cruel, lustful and a liar.

VIRGINIA: In a dream you bit your own thumb so violently were you arguing with an opponent. You have the temper of Dean Swift and would murder your wife. You would whizz a tea plate through a window.

LEONARD: [*quickly*] I expect Toby told you that. [*lower voice*] I'm sorry he died.

VIRGINIA: [*sharply*] We don't mention it. We've had too many deaths, my mother, my father, my half-sister Stella, then Toby. It's against our code to mourn.
[*She turns her back on him.*]

LEONARD: I have waited six years for you.

VIRGINIA: You seem so foreign, so disquietingly foreign.
[*she stamps her foot*]
No, I won't marry you. [*To the Audience*] Cruel . . . cru . . . el. I love cruelty. I could eat it on a spoon like malt and oil.
[VIRGINIA *turns round and walks downstage to the audience.*]

LEONARD: [*to Virginia, as if he were writing a letter*]
My dearest Virginia,
I must write you—I have not got any very clear

21

recollection of what I said to you this afternoon but I am sure you know why I came—I never realized how much I loved you until we talked about my going back to Ceylon. After that I could think about nothing else but you. I got into a state of hopeless uncertainty, whether you loved me or could ever love me or even like me.

VIRGINIA: There isn't anything really for me to say except that I should like to go on as before and that you should leave me free.

LEONARD: Something in you seems to rise up against me.

VIRGINIA: I pass from hot to cold in an instant and without any reason.

LEONARD: Apart from being in love with you it would be worth the risk of everything to marry you.

VIRGINIA: I love other people to have houses, mats, tables, chairs, pictures, china, tapestry over the four poster bed, lavender in chamber pots and biscuits in a tin should one waken hungry in the night. Other people in their vile little villas in the suburbs smelling of meat and humanity, all very dull and all very sensible. [As an aside]
Possibly your being a Jew comes into it, I feel no physical attraction for you. There are moments, when you kissed me, the other day was one, when I feel no more enraptured than a rock.

LEONARD: You have danced your marriage away, like Hippokliedes.

VIRGINIA: Like who?

LEONARD: Hippokliedes—he got rather above himself.

VIRGINIA: [smiling] Maybe I will marry you.

LEONARD: [turns and sees her smile.]

VIRGINIA: I only ask for someone to make me vehement and then I'll marry them.

LEONARD: Maybe I will make you vehement.

ACT ONE

VIRGINIA: I've got a disease you know, in the head. My pulse passes the limits of reason, goes insane. I walk making up phrases, I sit contriving scenes . . .

LEONARD: Some day you might write something astonishingly good.

VIRGINIA: And you?

LEONARD: I will earn my living in Fleet Street and write my masterpieces in the evening. [*he smiles*] Newspaper offices are paved with masterpieces.

VIRGINIA: We ask a great deal of life don't we.

LEONARD: Perhaps we shall get it.

[*Suddenly* VIRGINIA *takes off her mother's ring and gives it to him.*]

VIRGINIA: It was my mother's take it . . . don't ask me why.

LEONARD: Let's go to St. Pancras . . .

[*Thunder Storm*]

VIRGINIA: [*turns back to Audience*] Saved, saved by marriage, what a preposterous thing.

END OF SCENE TWO

ACT ONE

Scene Three

LEONARD: (V.O.) Whatever hour you woke there was a door shutting. From room to room they went, hand in hand, lifting here, opening there, making sure—a ghostly couple.
[clock]

VIRGINIA: [very rapid] Eleven o'clock, Twelve o'clock, thirteen, fourteen and so on, until they reach twenties and then thirties and then forties and fifties and sixties.

VIRGINIA: There is nothing to prevent them, phantoms of the foulest kind.

I hate this body . . . this belly . . . it's sordid . . . demand, mouth, food, lust, it's repulsive.

What enemy do we now perceive advancing against us.

Let the Jew speak.

To me all teaching and preaching is a blasphemy . . . communists, socialists, Roman Catholics, Rosicrucians . . . Fabians, think they can affect the destiny of nations.

If that's for me you know what to do with it, pooh, pooh, the goat is mad, the goat is not mad. And I am not mad. Mrs. Thackeray is mad. I know for instance that five hundred a year is considerably more valuable than beauty or rank. I am lazy, inane, gluttonous and the treatment is no good, [abrasive voice] I said the treatment is no good.

Committees, committees—committees for babies, committees for lunatics, a committee for the sick, the disabled and the dead.

[Pointing a finger at him]

Tell my why haven't you invented a committee for

25

the sane, because you don't want to. You are like one
of those mowing machines that go round and round
until finally their little square of corn is cut.
[*Laughing*] I have read your diary, I have cracked
your code, your Singhalese code, V—good fair or
bad day, good fair or bad night, as if I was a weather-
cock. [*Flauntingly*] There is no gate, no lock, no bolt
that you can set upon the freedom of my mind . . .
And for me neither, no gate, no lock, no bolt.
[*Vicious*]

LEONARD: Just one spoonful, just one.

VIRGINIA: It's disgusting, it's the entrail of pigs . . . it
oozes.

LEONARD: It's just arrowroot.

VIRGINIA: To be wise and to be happy. Those are the
hardest things.

LEONARD: You *are* wise and you are happy.

VIRGINIA: Suddenly how gentle you are. One of your
tricks.

Once you fall human nature is upon you. Human
nature is remorseless.

Call the nurse, call the doctor, call the do-gooders.
My mother's met them, she's just told me. She said
"Virginia, the dead are very boring and very con-
ventional, just like the living." What a chance the
British aristocracy had and lost it. I mean if they'd
grafted some brain onto those stupid bodies with
their housemaid sensibilities. And tell me, tell me
why do people make such a fuss about marriage and
copulation. Answer me. Such a stink. We didn't, did
we—we saw straight away that it was stupid, nasty,
phew.

That woman is laughing at me.

And are you buffetting against the gale, are you?

Get away from me, brute, I know what you want, I
know what you all want. One thing, I foretold the

murder of the Archduke and the death of Mrs. Robert Louis Stevenson, swine, brute, and I will not answer questions . . . [*forcing herself to be brave*] Yes, one must meet one's apparitions.

The violets are there and the daffodils.

Those books are stained, they're breeding, they're breeding mushrooms.

And the spiders are under my skirt. They're crawling up there, great long black . . . bestial.

[*She is now in real terror and like an animal.*]

VIRGINIA: You will put me away, people like you always do. With your blue books and your good causes, look at him, Mama, the man I married, the puppet. He said, [*turning to Leonard*] you said,

LEONARD: There is some primitive valve in our hearts, some primaeval cell in our brains, handed down to us from our reptillian, piscine or simian ancestors which makes us peculiarly primordially sensitive to the mother's death.

VIRGINIA: [*Hitting him.*] Thinking you can affect the destiny of nations you can't do anything for your wife, why am I like this? Because of you . . . yes I am inchoate. . . . Don't put me away, please don't put me away. It's so cold, it's so awful you have no idea, it's so far away. My mother, my mystery. Why am I talking to my mother? It's so cold.

Must muffle up against the night air. Must haul myself into this particular coat that belongs to me . . . Must, must.

Who are you?

[VIRGINIA *walks downstage*]

VIRGINIA: It was dreadful, dreadful. Two wasted, wearing years.

LEONARD: They are over. They are behind us now.

END OF ACT ONE

ACT TWO

Scene One

LEONARD: It's for your birthday.

VIRGINIA: [*timidly*] Shall I open it? Oh, it's beautiful. [*She opens it and takes out a beautiful green beaded bag with a chain handle. She puts it on her wrist.*]

VIRGINIA: Wouldn't Lady Dilke love it.

LEONARD: And you can look now. [VIRGINIA *turns around and sees the printing press.*]

LEONARD: It's a printing press. I got it in the Holborn viaduct for nineteen pounds, five shillings and fivepence.

VIRGINIA: What shall we do with it?

LEONARD: We shall print and we shall sell by subscription.

VIRGINIA: What shall we print? The k-aa-te sat on the m-aa-tte.

LEONARD: Come on, try it.

VIRGINIA: I'm afraid of it.

LEONARD: It will be good for you, something physical.

VIRGINIA: I know what I'll print—

There is no casement so magic as ours.

I shall tell you wonderful stories of the lunatics by and by. They elected me king and before I left I summoned a conclave and made a proclamation about Christianity.

I should hate to fail, I should hate to go under again—months, years, wiped out of one's life.

LEONARD: Here you are thinking, planning, printing, pressing forward, solid.

VIRGINIA: Let's gallop to it.

LEONARD: Kew Gardens by Virginia Woolf.

VIRGINIA: The Wise Virgins by Leonard Woolf. [*Airplane passes over.*]

29

VIRGINIA

LEONARD: Don't grind your teeth.

VIRGINIA: I don't want to die yet.

LEONARD: The chances are against it.

VIRGINIA: If so we shall be finished together.

LEONARD: One doesn't think of that.

VIRGINIA: No. One brews cocoa and waits for the boyscout to blow the bugle, to sound the all-clear.

LEONARD: [*reciting*] . . . breaking the silence with such depth of contentment, such passion of desire, or in the voices of children such freshness of surprise breaking the silence.

VIRGINIA: Will we have children?

LEONARD: Maybe . . . not.

VIRGINIA: Oh Mandrill.

LEONARD: Oh Mongoose.

VIRGINIA: I wrote to you every day.

[*Quoting*]

"Precious Mongoose, I lie and think of my special beast who does make me happy every day of my life."

LEONARD: And I read it every day.

VIRGINIA: And what else did Mongoose do?

LEONARD: At the weekends I walked on the downs near Aseham and I could hear the pounding of the guns on the Flanders field. I thought of my poor brothers, Cecil, and Philip, Rupert Brooke and all of them. I mind them being in the trenches and I mind being exempt and I hate this blasted shake of mine.

VIRGINIA: What would I do without you.

LEONARD: War changes nothing, it's just a costly muddle.

VIRGINIA: Mister Asquith says we are fighting for the moral forces of humanity . . .

LEONARD: Mister Asquith is a fool.

And that's hubristic patriotism. Nellie made a stew.

VIRGINIA: A nut stew.

LEONARD: Probably.

ACT TWO

VIRGINIA: I dream with rapture of roast mutton, don't
   you?

LEONARD: No, chocolate creams.

VIRGINIA: Or cold grouse and rough paté and pineapple
   chunks.

LEONARD: On Sunday we could go blackberrying.

VIRGINIA: When you eat toast you look like a rab-
   bit . . . Your nose twiches.
   Go on . . . eat it.
   [*Happily*]
   A wild rabbit. A king rabbit.
   A rabbit that makes laws for all other rabbits.
   [*Stretching her arms up*]
   This is life and I adore it.
   Lettuce, Rabbit?
   Come and take it out of my hand.
   Not a tame rabbit either.
   Lapin.

LEONARD: Simply and solely English, desiring melan-
   choly like most English people.

VIRGINIA: Lapin . . . lapin . . . king lapin . . . I am
   always finding new qualities in you, and every day I
   shall say, "And what did the King do today?"

LEONARD: "Today," said the King, twitching his nose as
   he lit his cigar, "today I chased a hare."
   "A woman hare."

VIRGINIA: A white hare, with big eyes.

LEONARD: Yes with eyes popping out of her head.

VIRGINIA: Aah . . . Lapinova.

LEONARD: Is that what she's called, Lapinova.

VIRGINIA: Yes, that's what she's called. She's wary and
   undependable whereas he is bold, and determined.
   They breed like rabbits.

LEONARD: Little devils. Shoot 'em. Jump on them with
   bog boots. So says the Squire.

VIRGINIA

VIRGINIA: Oh King Lapin if you weren't here and if your nose didn't twitch I should be miserable.

[*Telephone rings.*]

LEONARD: Not at home. Not at home.

[VIRGINIA *goes to answer the phone with a flourish.*]

VIRGINIA: Ah, the world wants us . . . how splendid. I like to feel important after writing . . . Writing quivers you.

[*She picks up the phone.*]

LEONARD: Say that we're going to the country.

VIRGINIA: Mrs. Woolf is not at home. She has gone to Capri. So has Mr. Woolf. He is meeting her in Capri.

[*She answers the phone.*]

Oh, Lady Colefax, Sybil, but how lovely. Perhaps we could, let me just ask.

[*She reaches over and whispers to Leonard.*]

It's for Wednesday. Arnold Bennett, Max Beerbohm, George Moore, Mr. Yeats.

[*He shakes his head to say no.*]

VIRGINIA: *(into the phone)* We should love it. It's what I've wanted so much. I've been leading the life of a badger. Yes, Wednesday.

[*She puts the phone down and speaks to Leonard, coaxing*]

LEONARD: You forget that on first meeting her she reminded you of the cherries on a servant's hat.

VIRGINIA: Now don't spout columns of fury at me. Be nice to Mongoose.

LEONARD: Everything has to be rationed, work, and walking and people and parties.

VIRGINIA: But you can't deny me my social side.

LEONARD: I mind when they drain you.

VIRGINIA: It's a trait I inherited from my mother—the joy of meeting people, being stimulated.

LEONARD: And dissipated.

VIRGINIA: Meeting people, taking the risk.

ACT TWO

LEONARD: Risks imply falls.

VIRGINIA: If we don't live venturously what is the point. We are like the most common animated little slugs.

VIRGINIA: On July the first the Woolfs had Philip and Irene Noel-Baker to tea . . .

LEONARD: And dined out.

VIRGINIA: On the second Lytton's sister Dorothy Bussy came to tea.

LEONARD: That evening was George Ryland's party.

VIRGINIA: The party at which Bertha Ruck performed. "Never let a sailor an inch above the knee." On July the third Raymond Mortimer and Hope Mirrilees dined at Tavistock Square.

LEONARD: Leo Myres and Daphne Sanger came in afterwards.

VIRGINIA: On July the fifth . . .

LEONARD: Sunday . . .

VIRGINIA: We went to a performance of *The Rehearsal*.

LEONARD: On the sixth Virginia dined with Clive.

VIRGINIA: Just to rub up my wits. On the ninth.

LEONARD: George Rylands . . .

VIRGINIA: Came to tea.

LEONARD: T. S. Eliot after dinner.

VIRGINIA: Pale marmorial Tom.

LEONARD: By midsummer the soirées and the worldy life dogged us.

VIRGINIA: Into the drawing room which was full, bright, miscellaneous. If one's normal pulse is seventy then in five minutes it was one hundred and twenty. And the blood not the sticky, white fluid of daytime but brilliant and prickly like champagne.

END OF SCENE ONE

33

ACT TWO

Scene Two

VIRGINIA: Shakespeare would have liked us tonight. Full of brio. Did you notice how Clive minced that little man, that little weasley man. I said, "Where's the Holy Ghost", and he said, "All around the sea". And I said, "The Holy Ghost, all around the sea?" and he said, "No, the whole coast".

LEONARD: I could have done without Mr. Yeats's disquisition on Fairies.

VIRGINIA: And you held up the proceedings of the soup with your fidgets.

[*Acting a stammer as she impersonates Mr. Bennett.*]

LEONARD: I was thinking up scientific forms of suicide for most of them there.

VIRGINIA: Particularly Mr. Arnold Bennett.

LEONARD: He said, "W . . . Woolf does n . . . not like my n . . . novels".

VIRGINIA: Oh but you did fidget, you were like this.

LEONARD: I came perilously close to ruining a tablecloth.

VIRGINIA: Stephen Tomlin is fleeing like Daphne from lovers, fleeing to where no one shall follow him. He's half crazy, wishing to love and to give, and finding—and this apalls him—that people love him in return. No one returns mine.

[VIRGINIA *nudges him. She is trying to get from him a reaction, a joke.*]

VIRGINIA: You liked Miss Gertrude Stein, you got on with her, throned on her broken seat. All of Edith Sitwell's furniture is derelict so to make up for that she is stuck about with jewels. Miss Stein, the swathed sausage, thinks *she* is the most intelligible and also the most popular writer in the world—"A rose is a rose is a rose". Is it? Despises people of English birth, come to think of it so do I. The charm of the young English woman eludes me. Eyes like dogs and great plaits down their backs and what pray did you make of Mrs. Nicolson, Miss Vita Sackville, mother, wife, great lady, hostess, and scribbler.

LEONARD: I didn't talk to her.

VIRGINIA: No need. She has a weak chin. I don't like women with moustaches. She's like an over-ripe grape. She writes twenty thousand words in a fort-night. She's a factory. An ancestor of theirs took the death warrant to Mary Stewart and so touched was she by the delicacy of his approach that she gave him a prayer book as a present. It's in the private chapel at Knowle, the family seat.

LEONARD: She is about to be disinherited and her mother's mad.

VIRGINIA: Just like you to get the facts.

[*He hands her a glass of milk but* VIRGINIA *disdains it.*]

VIRGINIA: Oh no, not milk and rest, not all that again.

[*She knocks on the table*]

Must, must, must, must sleep, must rest, no dining out, no gallivanting. Alone in my burrow.

[*He puts the milk a distance away.*]

VIRGINIA: Don't fuss me. Don't coop me up.

Love from Pot who's very hot.

[*Singing*]

"Never let a sailor an inch above the knee,"

What I think of is arriving and seeing Vita black and scarlet under a lamp.

Equanimity Mrs. Woolf, practice equanimity.

I shall be cold, I shall be hostile, I shall be indifferent.

Mrs. Nicolson.

[*She smiles.*]

The Hon. Mrs. Nicolson. Snob that I am, I trace
your passions five hundred years back and they
become romantic to me. I have a perfectly untrue but
romantic vision of you in my mind, stamping out the
hops in a great vat in Kent, stark naked . . .
[she laughs]
brown as a satyr and very beautiful. How long do
you take to milk on your great estate and how do you
cool it and do you churn and make butter. Facts Mrs.
Nicolson, facts.

Why am I talking to you. Simple I like to make you
up. I assure you I have every need of illusion. . . .

Oh Mrs. Nicolson, aren't you a card. Why didn't you
come in, why run away.

My own garden in Tavistock Square. What a treat.

I expect you're jealous. [To LEONARD] Why don't
you eat one . . . go on. Nibble a crocus.

[To VITA] You do, I suppose, disapprove of my
dress, my apparel.

VITA: It's dreadful.

VIRGINIA: I was advised by the Editor of Vogue, a Mrs.
Todd, to wear this. It cost me four guineas and look
at my gloves.

[She is not wearing gloves.]

VITA: Todd! So you whore after her.

VIRGINIA: Better whore after her than timidly copulate
with the Editor of the Times Literary Supplement.

VITA: So long as one goes the whole hog.

VIRGINIA: Oh. Mrs. Nicolson . . . Do you cut up
rough, like a baroness.

VITA: I would say not as rough as you. You see people,
but you don't feel them . . . We, they, are all
material to you.

VIRGINIA: In that case let's stick to literature, it's sim-
pler. For instance one test of poetry is that without
saying things, indeed saying the opposite, it conveys

things. I read Crabbe and I think of fens, marshes, shingle, rivers . . . But there is nothing of the sort. There is how Lucy got engaged to Edward Shore.

VITA: You should wear shorter skirts and show off your shins.

VIRGINIA: They are not my best point.

VITA: Captious aren't you?

VIRGINIA: And you, what are you?

VITA: A woman—yes, but a million other things. A snob? Ancestors—proud of them. Greedy, luxurious, vicious, don't care a damn. Like lying in bed on fine linen listening to the pigeons.

VIRGINIA: Like giving pain.

VITA: Silver, victuals, wine, maids, footmen, spoilt perhaps.

VIRGINIA: You are so much in full sail, on the high tide.

VITA: When shall I take you there?

VIRGINIA: Where?

VITA: Home, to Long Barn.

VIRGINIA: I shall see a table laid with jugs of chocolate and buns.

VITA: You shall sit beneath the arras, you shall eat game and there will be fireworks down by the frozen pond.

VIRGINIA: [marvelling] Ottoline took me motoring one night here in London and the effect was stupendous—St. Paul's, Tower Bridge, moonlight, the river. Ottoline in full dress and paint, white and gaudy like a tombstone, all the hoppers and bargees coming home drunk. It was the Bank Holiday. Sometimes London can be very vivid. I was on the top of a bus going to Waterloo and there was an old beggar woman blind, in Kingsway, holding a mongrel in her arms and singing. There was a recklessness about her.

VITA: Just say when.

ACT TWO

VIRGINIA: [*to the audience*] I am not sure that I am not throwing myself overboard.

VITA: [*very sportingly*] What used we young fellows in the cockpit of the Marie Rose say about a woman who threw herself overboard. Ah, we had a word for her.

VIRGINIA: Ah, we must omit that word, it is disrespectful in the extreme.

VITA: Shall we say Tuesday?

VIRGINIA: I shall let Leonard decide that. [*To* LEONARD] I am growing old and want more mustard with my meat.

[VITA *and* VIRGINIA *come downstage*]

I'm crack-brained . . . sometimes I am not Virginia at all.

VITA: And now?

VIRGINIA: Now I am a little drunk . . . this wine for instance, I see it as amber . . . and the beams are swaying and it's bliss, and I find you one of the nicest and most magnanimous of women.

VITA: Catch.

VIRGINIA: You say you esteem me. That's damn cold. Still, I accept it like the humble servant I am.

VIRGINIA: (V.O.) She has found me, she has kissed me, all is shattered.

VITA: Good God, you are not going to give me chastity. The whole edifice of female government and wiliness is based on that foundation stone. Women are not chaste.

VIRGINIA: Do you know that from your husband?

VITA: I know it from my experience as a man.

VIRGINIA: Were you?

VITA: Yes.

[*Like a knight falls on one knee and speaks in a cavalier voice.*]

Falling on his knees, the Archduke Harry made the

most passionate declaration of his suit. He told her that he had something like twenty million ducats in a strong box at his castle. He had more acres than any nobleman in England. The shooting was excellent. He could promise her a mixed bag of Ptarmigan and grouse such as no English moor or Scottish either could rival. True, the pheasants had suffered from the gape in his absence and the does had slipped their young.

VIRGINIA: [*in the same vein*] As he spoke enormous tears formed in his violet eyes.

VITA: [*unable to resist laughing*] But that don't count. Want to eat?

VIRGINIA: Can't eat.

VITA: A little of the fat, ma'am?

VIRGINIA: Not yet, ma'am.

VITA: Would you like to play Fly Loo?

VIRGINIA: What is it?

VITA: It's gambling. Great sums of money can be lost and if you lose you will have to marry me.

VIRGINIA: Show me.

VITA: I bet you . . .
That a fly will land on this lump of sugar. Now you choose your lump.
[VIRGINIA *hesitates and then points to the one and then they both look around expecting flies. VITA snapes her fingers impatiently.*]

VITA: C'mon, flies, bluebottles, c'mon . . . don't be so sluggish.

VIRGINIA: I expect they're asleep, it's winter.

VITA: We'll change that.
[VITA *lets out a whistle as she dashes from one corner to another to try and arouse them.*]

VIRGINIA: Life and a lover. It does not scan.

VITA: [*acting voice*] Dammit Madam, you are loveliness incarnate.

ACT TWO

VIRGINIA: Trembled. Turned hot. Turned cold.

VITA: [*still acting voice*] For she smiled the involuntary smile which women smile when their own beauty seems not their own.

Confronts them all of a sudden in a glass. And then she listened and heard only the leaves blowing and the sparrows twittering and then she sighed, life and a lover, it does not scan.

VIRGINIA: Would you like to crack a man over the head and tell him he lies in his teeth.

VITA: A pox on them I say.

VIRGINIA: And then she turned on her heel with extraordinary rapidity, whipped her emeralds from her neck.

VITA: Stripped her satin from her back.

VIRGINIA: Stood erect in her neat black silk knickerbockers and . . . *(does it)*

rang the bell.

[*The bell or gong is heard to ring throughout the house. No one answers it.*]

VITA: We are alone.

VIRGINIA: Let us go.

END OF SCENE TWO

ACT TWO

Scene Three

LEONARD: Virginia.

VITA: She said that you might be interested. Not that I think she likes it. She says there is something in my writing that doesn't vibrate. She *is* devillish.

LEONARD: She can be devillish. [*pause*]
She can be many things. She says her soft crevices are lined with hooks.

VITA: How did you propose to Virginia?

LEONARD: The usual way.

VITA: And did she accept, in the usual way? Or did she . . . demur?

LEONARD: First she said no. Then on the twenty ninth of May I was having lunch with her in her room when suddenly she told me that she *would* marry me. We took a train to Maidenhead and I hired a boat and rowed up the river to Marlow. Then we came back and dined at a restaurant, a riverside restaurant. In all it was ten hours. We seemed to drift through a beautiful vivid dream.

VITA: I can just imagine it.

LEONARD: Such moments are only moments, they pass in a flash. Before one knows it one is again of the herd.

VITA: I think she enjoyed her stay at Long Barn.

LEONARD: [*coldly*] I'm sure she did. She says you lavish on her the maternal protection that she most always wishes from everyone.

VITA: [*sharply*] So what is the danger then?

LEONARD: She has to lead a quiet, almost vegetative life.

VITA: She says to live venturously is the thing.

LEONARD: You don't know her. She leaves the ground, she follows her voices. She stumbles after them.

VITA: And what do they tell her?

LEONARD: Everything. She goes through every stage. She goes beyond reach.

VITA: Are you asking me to give her up?

LEONARD: I am telling you to be careful.

VITA: But she is an exquisite companion, vulnerable, sensitive, and for the record, I do love her.

LEONARD: Backstairs?

VITA: It's a spiritual thing, an intellectual thing. She inspires a feeling of tenderness.

LEONARD: Her terror is of going mad again.

VITA: She has told me some of your life together . . . she was quite open about it.

LEONARD: You may think that you have guessed our troubles but for each of us there is something more, something deeper.

VITA: As with me and Harold . . . for each of us the other is the magnetic north. So let's not quibble about things.

[VIRGINIA *can be seen coming towards the door.*]

LEONARD: It's not just playing with fire.

VITA: Oh, but how satisfying if it loosens the liniaments.

VIRGINIA: I've been to the dentist. I say to him "Why do you do this to me?" and he says "Mrs. Woolf your skin is the most sensitive in all London." [*Feeling her skin.*] I daresay it is. Leonard paints my skin with zinc ointment which I lick. I daresay it's poisonous and I shall be dead. [*Turning to the cluttered table.*] Shall we have tea?

LEONARD: I've got to go to Hampstead to a meeting.

VIRGINIA: [*sarcastically*] Oh, what is to be the big subject today—the Dye stuff Bill, the thyroid gland, the freedom of the marriage couch. [*To Vita*] His

44

secretary is like a chest of drawers, and his mother, Mrs. Woolf Senior, keeps a basket of undarned socks next to her bed so that when she wakens she can darn them straight away. That's where Leonard got his application.

LEONARD: [to Vita] Virginia is at her best when she is in wrath.

[He goes out. VIRGINIA and VITA stand and look at each other, each for the other an object of desire.]

VIRGINIA: [tentatively] Well.

VITA: Well.

VIRGINIA: I left a nightgown behind and a grisly powder puff.

VITA: Buffles has sent them on . . . Was quite impressed with you . . . he'd seen your photo in The Listener.

VIRGINIA: Does he ever catch you in the act?

VITA: No.

VIRGINIA: Your husband wrote to me.

VITA: Yes he said he would.

VIRGINIA: [reading]"I am glad that Vita has come under an influence so stimulating and so sane. [She lets out a hoot of laughter.]
You need never worry about my having any feelings except a longing that Vita's life should be as rich and as sincere as possible. I loath jealousy as I loath all forms of disease."

VITA: You and I must be the two happiest married women in all of London.

VIRGINIA: But the soul is by nature unmated, is it not?

VITA: You look ravishing.

VIRGINIA: I feel like some dowdy decrepit horrible dingy old fly.

VITA: [coyly] Fishing are you?

VIRGINIA: Come to demoralise me?

VITA: Yes, darling, to haunt your terrace.

VIRGINIA: Isn't it like living in a damp dustbin?

VITA: Yes a bit commonplace but good for the chastity.

VIRGINIA: Bad Vita. Bad wicked Vita. I will keep Tuesday free for any purpose you like.

VITA: And what have you been doing since, Mrs. Woolf?

VIRGINIA: All manner of things. Thinking—Your moonlight. Your barking stags. I felt like a piece of wood this morning and I thought about that.

VITA: I have come to say au revoir.

VIRGINIA: First the close dry sensation of being wood, then the grinding of storm, then the slow delicious ooze of the sap. Au revoir? Where are you going?

VITA: To join Harold in Persia.

VIRGINIA: I have no time for people in ambassadorial states. A lot of humbug and falseness.

VITA: I have no time for them either. I don't go to those functions but I do go to my husband.

VIRGINIA: So you have the wanderlust again.

VITA: To see my husband.

VIRGINIA: When do you go?

VITA: [*rising*] Don't take it badly.

VIRGINIA: Of course not, we gain as much as we lose by this sort of thing.

[VITA *goes*]

I suppose I could read Doris Dagliesh and see what it's like to have nerves and live in Wandsworth with one's mother.

Or think of Katherine Mansfield—"Do not quite forget me," she said in her ice-cold wreath, sometimes she would kiss me—would look at me as if her eyes would like to be always faithful. For our friendship was a real thing, we said, looking at each other quite straight. It would always go on whatever happened. [*cross voice*]

Miss Katherine Mansfield smelling like a civet cat.

ACT TWO

Gone and left me in a pucker.

Now you are arriving driving into the gates of Teheran. There's Harold coming out to meet you. There you sit proud as a peacock. My God, to be with you and the fourteen cream-coloured ponies and the young mare and the lighted window in the fishmonger's at Sevenoaks. Now you are stopping at some place for figs and wine, you are very excited all in a whirl, like a flock of birds flying about. Yes you are an agile animal—no doubt about it . . . heart you have none.

I want to know particularly, among a crowd of other things, have you talked to Harold about giving up silk stockings and swords and gold lace and humbug and nonsense. Harold is a happy man and I am an envious woman. I cannot hold out hopes that you are thinking of me.

By the way Leonard thinks your dog is a hermaphrodite. I didn't tell you but we went to Violet Bonham Carter's last night, or did I. Philip Ritchie told me I was the chief coquette in London, no, "Allumeuse" Clive corrected him. [*In sharper voice.*] Allumeuse.

Then my suspenders came down, dragging with them an old rag of chemise—why didn't you tell me one must fasten one's suspenders properly. Always some misery like suspenders to clip my wings of glory and good God I must buy a hat. How are you? Any malaria? I'm so solitary . . . my brain a whirlygig, in bed at night, as I walk the streets, everywhere, in the lamplight, you in your emeralds.

We are still here talking about love and sodomy. Morgan Foster says he's worked it out and one spends three hours on food, six on sleep, four on work, two on love. Lytton say ten on love. I say the whole day on love. I say it's seeing things through a

47

VIRGINIA

purple shade. "But you've never been in love," they say.

It's true the other night I did take a glass too much. It's your fault though. Bobo Mayer is a great seducer in her way.

Yes I am shingled or rather bingled. We went to see Keats's house and I sat in the room where Keats wrote his odes and saw the engagement ring he gave Fanny Brawne. We'll go there in a tram but it will be May. Instantly all the lights go up and the whole tram becomes gold and rosy. Damned lustrous face of yours. I wish to God I'd asked you to wire.

VITA: (V.O.) Come to Greece. Join us there. I leave it to your imagination to guess what it would mean to me if I saw you coming down the gangplank.

VIRGINIA: What would it mean to you if you saw me coming down the gangplank. What would it mean to me? [*harsher voice*]

What would happen if I let myself over a precipice—marked V? No I won't come. I shall stay here and write about it. That shall be my victory. Ain't people cussed.

Orlando. A Biography.

Stuck a pair of pistols in her belt, finally wound about her person several strings of emeralds and pearls of the finest orient which had formed part of the ambassadorial wardrobe.

LEONARD: This done she leant out of the window, gave one low whistle and descended the shattered and bloodstained staircase . . .

VIRGINIA: There in the shadow of a giant fig tree waited an old Gypsy on a donkey. He led another by the bridle. Orlando swung her leg over it and thus attended by a lean dog, riding a donkey in the company of a gypsy, left Constantinople.

ACT TWO

LEONARD: They rode for several days and nights and met with a variety of adventures . . .

VIRGINIA: Some at the hands of men some at the hands of nature.

LEONARD: For women are not obedient, chaste scented and exquisitely apparelled by nature. They can only attain these graces without which they may enjoy one of the delights of life by the most serious discipline.

VIRGINIA: Is it bad? Is it rubbish? Is it slovenly?

LEONARD: It's different—it's spry.

VIRGINIA: I began it as a joke.

LEONARD: It will keep them guessing.

VIRGINIA: [*tenderly*] The consequence of not always being with one's husband is that one begins to talk and write nonsense.

LEONARD: I predict that it will sell.

VIRGINIA: And we shall buy a house in the country and put down a pair of trees. What I like about the country is that I can read there. So divine to come in from a walk to have tea by the fire and read and read, say *Othello*, say anything.

LEONARD: But even if Shakespeare or Montaigne should knock on the door we shall pretend to be out.

[VITA *re-enters*]

VIRGINIA: You see I would not have married you had I not preferred living with you to anyone else.

VITA: My darling. I am in no state to write to you, I can't say anything except that I am completely dazzled, bewitched, enchanted, under a spell. I feel like one of those wax figures in a shop, on which you have hung a robe stitched with jewels. It is like being alone in a dark room with a treasure chest full of rubies and nuggets and brocades.

[LEONARD *picks up a small diary, reads it and laughs.*]

LEONARD: Do you want to hear what our factotum of-

49

fice boy is saying about us. [*quoting*] "Orlando" is selling like hot cakes. LW, Svengali, is terrified we will run out of stock and it's my job to count the copies and put them into packages. Mrs. W. has brought a very smart winter outfit, long, Russian style, black, cossack coat of astrakhan and a Russian hat.

VITA: Also you have invented a new form of narcissism. I confess—I am in love with Orlando—a complication I hadn't foreseen. Virginia my dearest, I can only thank you.

VIRGINIA: Vita my dear, unless you are as I think all my friends are, something I dreamt.

Coins in my pocket, how luxurious. Soon I shall be as well-paid as a Civil Servant.

LEONARD: How would you like to be picked up out of here and set down in one of the wildest moors in England.

VIRGINIA: To see the eclipse.

LEONARD: Darker and darker.

[*The stage is completely dark and the sun invisible.*]

VIRGINIA: Like the birth of the world.

LEONARD: The earth is dead.

VIRGINIA: How does the light return to the world.

LEONARD: Miraculously, later normally, always with a great sense of relief.

END OF SCENE THREE

50

ACT TWO

Scene Four

Gardening

The country. Bird song.

VIRGINIA: A nightingale?

LEONARD: No . . . a daybird.

VIRGINIA: Chuckling over the succulence of worms, snails and grit. I stayed up too late.

LEONARD: Everyone liked your play.

VIRGINIA: Fresh Water—a farce. I should have taken my bow on a donkey.

LEONARD: The children loved it. They loved the tribes of elves and the baying ape.

VIRGINIA: Who was that elderly virgin Clive brought—With stationary eyes like an oyster.

LEONARD: A Miss Buchanan. She's from Cheltenham.

VIRGINIA: Women like her have no reason to exist, in this world or in the next.

LEONARD: Maynard is back from America. He says it is an impossible climate . . . it has collected all the faults of all the climates and nobody could produce a great work there.

VIRGINIA: Because of the climate! He says I live and write in an opium dream.

LEONARD: Old Maynard. The doughty defier of God. Quite stingy, he and Lydia, two grouse for eleven people.

VIRGINIA: I left my shawl at Nessa's. I always leave something. You say women cry—I don't know why I cry, mostly with Nessa or why I criticize her children. Perhaps her progeny drew us asunder. Yet I love them. You see I am undependable.

LEONARD: Did I tell you I met George Bernard Shaw in

51

Longacre the other day and he said he was inspired to write Heartbreak House when he first met you.

VIRGINIA: He doesn't like me, he doesn't like what I write—too vapid, not practical enough and not partial. Wyndham Lewis doesn't like me either.

LEONARD: That is just the usual litter of undergraduate venom.

VIRGINIA: [*sharply*] "I am a peeper not a looker. I am fundamentally prude." There is a queer disreputable pleasure in being abused, in being a martyr, having one's back to the wall. I shall write a pamphlet On Being Despised.

LEONARD: They cannot touch you, only as a robin can affect a rhinoceros.

VIRGINIA: The subject of her writing was the little world of people like herself, a small class, a dying class, a class with inherited privileges, private incomes and sheltered lives.

LEONARD: I ought to show them our outside privy. Frozen-fingered, frozen-hearted, university specialists.

VIRGINIA: Perhaps we moderns lack love, our torture makes us writhe.

LEONARD: Look . . . the pear tree is swagged with fruit.

VIRGINIA: I should have had children, Leonard. I should have had. I am angry with myself for not having taken the risk. Carrington bears none of Duncan's children, nor Alex any of James's, nor Frances—ain't it odd how all the flowers of female youth and spent-youth will die with their buds unopened.

LEONARD: You have nephews, nieces, oodles of friends, you say if I meet one more person I will pullulate.

VIRGINIA: You were afraid for me weren't you. Never mind, I distrust the maternal passion . . . it is immeasurable and unscrupulous and destructive and limiting.

LEONARD: It is not a world for children anymore. The die is cast. It is now a question, an impending question, of war versus peace, ugliness versus beauty, civilization versus savagery.

VIRGINIA: Love versus lust.

LEONARD: Inevitably defrauding ourselves.

VIRGINIA: Leonard, have you never wanted a Lavinia or a Jane or a Geraldine or a Penelope?

LEONARD: No, only a Virginia.

VIRGINIA: Grey as a scullery pail and her hair falls in the soup.

LEONARD: And she writes in the mould of eternity.

VIRGINIA: Nonsense. Crumbs, Variations, Possibilities, Bad shots.

LEONARD: Supple, naked and always to the truth.

VIRGINIA: And you?

LEONARD: Too much facts, too hidebound.

VIRGINIA: I cried when you made your speech at the Labour Party Conference. Mr. Bevin's attack on Landbury was dramatic but too vitriolic, too grasping.

LEONARD: I thought I was a bit artificial . . . the battered man hawking his conscience about.

VIRGINIA: Do you think that.

LEONARD: I think that we like carrying our private cross.

VIRGINIA: I have sucked so much of your time and your sap.

[*A car is heard offstage. She backs away.*]

Who is that? Maybe it is Nessa, maybe she's bringing my shawl back. Old Nessa, old dolphin shuts me out. Oh she does. She detests emotion.

[*Leonard comes in.*]

LEONARD: It is a journalist.

VIRGINIA: A what?

LEONARD: He says you made an appointment, he rang earlier.

VIRGINIA: I thought it was the vet about the cow's sciatica. I can't. I won't. I will not rub my face in that pail of offal.

[VIRGINIA *runs towards a corner of the room in fear. Leonard goes out.*]

He'd come in here and get his little notebook out and cross his legs and think "attacked as a feminist, hinted at as a sapphoist" . . . better butter her up, (mimicking him) Mrs. Woolf it is said that you have remoulded the English language. How do you feel about that and how do you cope with the celebrity business? I don't know. I detest the hardness of old age. I am an elderly, dowdy, fussy, ugly, incompetent woman. I am tired. I can make bread. I invent menus. [*Confessional voice.*] Gradually he would winkle it out of me—up at eight, wash, breakfast, out to my garden shed for three hours. Lunch at one, rissoles—or halibut, then custard, and a smoke, then into thick shoes and take my dog Pinka on his lead and up the hill to the shepherd's cottage, or the Piddinghoe farm back home along the river, tea at four, letter writing . . . [*stronger voice*] Queer, the contraction of life to a village radius. Very small beer. In London now I'd be owling through the streets. More pack and thrill than here. Our habits, our apparitions, these things you see me by, these are pretences . . . Beneath it is all dark and it is spreading . . .

[LEONARD *comes in and she emerges from her hiding.*]

LEONARD: He has gone. He was with his wife.

VIRGINIA: I hope they enjoyed the hedgerows.

ACT TWO

[*The voice of Chamberlain announcing the outbreak of the War.*]

LEONARD: So this is it.

VIRGINIA: What do we do now.

LEONARD: Our lovely country destroyed.

VIRGINIA: Our manorhouses, our moats, our downs. Will they cross the Channel?

LEONARD: Who knows. Hitler has a million men armed and it's not for summer manoeuvers.

VIRGINIA: What do we do now?

LEONARD: We wait and we go on discussing the new room or the new chair or the new book or the new cistern.

VIRGINIA: How tired I am of stories, how tired I am of phrases that come down beautifully with their feet on the ground . . . and die like stars.

END OF SCENE FOUR

ACT TWO

Scene Five

The Country.

Six months later.

[VIRGINIA *is in her room. It is near evening, and she has been writing and she is very restless.*]

VIRGINIA: I begin now to forget, I begin to doubt the fixity of tables, the reality of here and now, to tap my knuckles smartly upon the edges of solid objects and say "Are you hard." I have been so many different things, have made so many different sentences, all lost in the process of eating and drinking. And now I ask "Who am I?"

I was crossing the stream when . . .

The stream at the bottom of the garden where our wood meets the Black Wood.

Catching colds, no not again, night travelling and cream and stars and continental railways and Brad-shaw . . . catching cold, catching cold and rheumatism . . . not again.

Must prepare dinner. Fish forgotten . . . so what shall it be . . . tripe and onions.

It's heavenly here. L and I alone. [*she picks up a rug.*] And all the clothes-drudgery and all the social drudgery obliterated. I will never dine with Lady Dilke again or give a prize to a French-woman, I went to London yesterday. [*she puts the rug over her shoulder. Sadder voice.*] All my old squares gashed, dismantled, the red bricks all white powder, like a builder's yard. [*Braver voice.*] I said to my horses "Home John," My cohorts will see me through.

VIRGINIA: What cohorts Virginia, what cohorts.
Is that you Leonard, is that you?

Can't be you yet. Maybe it's Nessa. Is that you
Nessa.
The downs were like lions today . . .
couchant . . . yellow, unstained . . . you could paint
them.
Nessa, don't shut me out. Don't say "Virginia lives in
a world of her own," Virginia wants you here now,
you and Leonard, the two people I love most.
Brilliant amorous day was divided as sheerly from the
night as land from water. [*practical voice*] Nessa I
need you. Vita I need you. Tell me you are soon
coming. I want to sink into your arms, to feel the
festival and the firelight.
Dinner, halibut. You're late, Leonard. No trains, no
cars, no petrol, no butter. All our friends isolated
over winter fires or in the bomb sites. [*to the
audience*] Yes, London was full of queues, children
and women, queueing for the air raid shelter with
their bags and their blankets. Carpets nailed to
windows, ceilings down, rubble. [*Suddenly thought-
ful and in a sharper voice*] Leonard, why aren't you
back? Perhaps you're . . . No you're not, they don't
raid till night and our private luck has not run out.
Leave me. I did nothing to deserve you . . .
nothing . . . Far from it. [*She points to the window
and beyond.*] Our luck has not turned. Our pear tree
is bearing fruit and I am a red admiral feasting on
an apple.
And I am filling my mind with the
Elizabethans—"Hang there like fruit my soul until
the tree doth die." Who will be killed tonight . . . not
us, I say.
Dawn is some sort of whitening of the sky, some sort
of renewal, another day, another Friday, another
20th March . . . I'm not responsible for the world, I
am *not* responsible.

ACT TWO

[LEONARD *enters*]

Ah, there you are, just in time . . . I have dinner ready. A moment of great household triumph. Yes I am a little triumphant.

LEONARD: Who were you talking to just now?

VIRGINIA: You know me, tongue always clacking.

LEONARD: But not so fast.

VIRGINIA: [*rapidly*] A new book pumping in the brain. My mind is agape and red-hot with it. It's in here [*taps her head*] stored. I shall scrape the sea bed, clean.

Those are mine.

LEONARD: Our house was bombed, the whole square was bombed last night.

VIRGINIA: Funny that I didn't know, that I didn't guess.

LEONARD: It's still smouldering. Miss P. salvaged what she could. She was in overalls sweeping up everything. She didn't want you to be upset.

VIRGINIA: And the press?

LEONARD: It's damaged but it's not ruined. We're going to move to Letchworth tomorrow.

VIRGINIA: Is the house completely gone?

LEONARD: Yes. Just a great pile of brick and glass everywhere. [*As he hands them to her.*] I brought your diaries.

VIRGINIA: [*on a happy note*] I feel quite exhilarated really at losing everything. It's like starting again, quite bare. [*reading*] "A tree pelted with starlings."

E for Ephesus, U for Unicorn, S for Syntax.

LEONARD: [*worried*] Virginia?

VIRGINIA: [*very rapidly*] No, not leaving the ground, not this time, staying with feet on the ground.

LEONARD: Shouldn't we see a doctor. You like our new doctor.

But you like Octavia, she's our friend.

VIRGINIA: There's nothing the matter with me. [*Pouting*

59

like a child.] She'll order a rest cure, I'll be sent away from Mongoose.

LEONARD: Only if it's necessary.

VIRGINIA: [*firmly*] It's not necessary. It's nothing. You were late. I was worried. Paralysed. It was all so silent here.

LEONARD: I'm sorry. There was a bomb scare at Richmond, and we all got out, then we went to Croydon, there was a siren there, we all got out, we had to wait for the All Clear. [*humorously*] I couldn't find a public lavatory.

VIRGINIA: [*wistfully*] "Then above the little grave we kissed again with tears."

LEONARD: Virginia, are you sure?

VIRGINIA: Yes, quite sure. I've got to start again on a book. This one has to be damned deep, the deepest of my adventures. No babble. No glibness. Something new in my pot . . .

We had our own little drama here today. [*joyous voice*] The river burst its banks.

LEONARD: I saw it, walking home. It's like the sea . . . it's white and misty.

VIRGINIA: Dear old nature kicking her heels up.

LEONARD: It even smelt like the sea.

VIRGINIA: So my marsh walk is gone.

LEONARD: Only for a day or so, until they mend the bank.

VIRGINIA: The haystacks were in flood . . . sailing about . . . like the toy boats in Hyde Park so long ago . . . the water roaring through the gap in the hill. Poor Londoners with another night to face. Oh the freedom . . . of here.

LEONARD: I won't go up tomorrow.

VIRGINIA: Oh yes you will. You see, I like my Mongoose going and I can think of him doing all the things he has to do, seeing the move of the press, talking to Miss P. . . . and getting me some books from the London Library.

LEONARD: You would say if you were, jangled.

VIRGINIA: I have never been so well. You see the old hunger for books is on me, the childish passion, so that I am very "happy" as the saying is. Leonard, let us walk in the moonlight and see our own inland sea. We can walk along the edge and work up an appetite.

LEONARD: [*taking her arm*] And if a raid comes a haystack is a very good thing to hide behind.

END OF SCENE FIVE

ACT TWO

Scene Six

The Country.

VIRGINIA: And in me too the wave rises. It swells, it arches its back, it is death . . . Death is the enemy. [*practical voice*] Hurry, hurry.

Terrible if he came back, if anyone came in, the maid or the gardener, at the very last minute.

My hair flying back like a young man's, like Percival's.

Against you I will fling myself unvanquished and unyielding . . . oh death.

LEONARD: Virginia!

[*reading*]

Dearest—

I feel certain that I am going mad again. I feel we can't go through another of those terrible times. And I shan't recover this time. I begin to hear voices and I can't concentrate. So I am doing what seems the best thing to do.

VIRGINIA: You have been in every way all that anyone could be. I don't think two people could have been happier till this terrible disease came. I can't fight any longer. I know that I am spoiling your life, that without me you can work. And you will, I know. You see, I can't even write this properly. If anybody could have saved me it would have been you. Everything has gone from me.

LEONARD: We did not find her body for two weeks. Some children found her washed up near Lewes. There were heavy stones in the pocket of her jacket, it was terrible, it was the most terrible thing.

VIRGINIA: I leant over the edge of the boat and fell down. I went under the sea. I have been dead and yet am now alive again—it was awful, awful and as before waking. [*Her voice gets quicker and quicker.*] The voices of the birds and the sound of the wheel chime and chatter, in a queer harmony, grow louder and louder and the sleeper feels himself drawing towards the shores of life, the sun growing hotter, cries sounding louder, something tremendous about to happen.